the facts about
FLOWERING PLANTS

Rebecca Hunter

First published in 2003 by Franklin Watts
Franklin Watts, 96 Leonard Street, London EC2A 4XD

Franklin Watts Australia
45–51 Huntley Street, Alexandria, NSW 2015
This edition published under license from Franklin Watts.
All rights reserved.

Editor: Rebecca Hunter; Design: Keith Williams; Consultant:
Jeremy Bloomfield; Illustrations: Peter Bull: page 4, 9, 13–14

Published in the United States by Smart Apple Media
1980 Lookout Drive, North Mankato, Minnesota 56003

Library of Congress Cataloging-in-Publication Data

Hunter, Rebecca (Rebecca K. de C.)
The facts about flowering plants / Rebecca Hunter.
p. cm. "First published in 2003 by Franklin Watts ...
London" — T.p. verso.
Contents: Flowering plants—Seeds—The growing plant—
Stems and roots—Leaves—Flowers—Pollination—Animal
pollination—From pollen to seed—Life cycle of a sunflower—
Special adaptations—Unusual flowers—Plants and people.
ISBN 1-58340-454-6
1. Plants—Juvenile literature. 2. Angiosperms—Juvenile
literature. [1. Plants. 2. Angiosperms.] I Title: Flowering
plants. II. Title.

QK49.H87 2004
580—dc22   2003060119

9 8 7 6 5 4 3 2 1

Photographs:
Bruce Coleman Collection: page 4, 8 (Tore Hagman), 9
(Hans Reinhard), 10 bottom (Joy Langsbury), 11 (Jeff Foott),
15 top (Jules Cowan), 18 top (Joe McDonald), bottom left
(Kim Taylor), 21 top (Jane Burton), 25 top right (Jane Burton);
Discovery Picture Library: page 6 all, 10 top, 20, 22;
Oxford Scientific Films: page 7, 12 (Breck P Kent), 13
bottom (Bob Gibbons), 14, 16 (Richard Packwood), 17
bottom, 18 bottom right (Bert & Babs Wells), 19 (Bob
Gibbons), 21 bottom (Harold Taylor), 23 top (Martyn
Chillmaid), 23 bottom, 24 (Stan Osolinski), 25 bottom
(Carlos Sanches Alonso), 26, 27 (Deni Brown), 28 top, 28
bottom (Max Gibbs), 29 (Mark Hamblin); **Photodisc**: cover,
page 5, 13 top, 15 bottom, 17 top, 25 top left.

the facts about
FLOWERING PLANTS

Contents

Words in **bold** appear in the glossary on page 30.

Flowering plants

We live in a world that is full of plants. The largest group of plants are those that produce flowers.

The plant kingdom is made up of two groups of plants: those that produce flowers and those that do not. Most plants belong in the group of flowering plants.

Non-flowering plants

Non-flowering plants include mosses, lichens, and ferns. These are small, low-growing plants that have no root systems or flowers. They produce spores instead of seeds. **Coniferous** trees such as pines, cedars, and firs produce cones instead of flowers. The seeds grow inside the cones.

▼ Trees are flowering plants. This apple tree in full blossom stands in a field of dandelions.

Flowering plants

When you imagine flowering plants, you probably first think about the brightly-colored flowers that are planted in gardens and parks or grow wild in fields. However, flowering plants form a very large group and include many **species** that you may have not thought of.

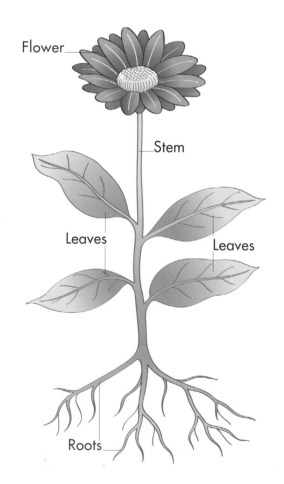

▲ The main parts of a flowering plant.

All broad-leaved trees are flowering plants. They include oak trees, beech trees, willows, and many other trees. They are known as broad-leaved trees because their leaves are broad and flat, unlike the sharp needles on coniferous trees.

Other flowering plants include fruit trees, vegetables, herbs, and grasses. Many grasses such as wheat, barley, and sweetcorn are grown for food.

We all love looking at the bright colors and smelling the pleasant scents of flowers, but plants do not produce flowers for our pleasure. Flowers have a very important role ensuring that the next generation of plants will grow.

▲ A meadow full of flowering plants, with non-flowering conifers in the background.

key facts

- The plant kingdom is divided into flowering and non-flowering plants.

- There are more types of flowering plants than non-flowering plants.

- Flowering plants include broad-leaved trees, grasses, vegetables, weeds, and herbs.

Seeds

Nearly all flowering plants develop from seeds. Each seed contains an embryo (the young plant) and a store of food to help the embryo develop.

Fruits and nuts

Seeds grow inside the part of a plant called a fruit. We can identify the seeds of edible fruit quite easily. Think of the seeds inside a lemon or the stone inside a cherry. Some foods that we call vegetables, such as tomatoes and cucumbers, should really be called fruits

◀▲ The seeds of a tomato or lemon are inside the fruit. The strawberry's seeds are on the outside.

because they contain seeds. Beans and peas belong to a group called legumes. Legumes produce their seeds inside a long casing called a pod.

A nut is a seed that is covered in a dry, hard-cased fruit. Acorns, hazelnuts, walnuts, and coconuts are all really the seeds of their trees.

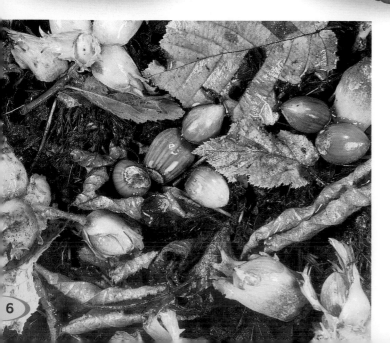

◀ These nuts are the fruit of the hazel tree.

You can do it...

See how seeds germinate by growing fava beans. Line the sides of a jar with blotting paper. Put a few fava beans between the paper and the glass. Add a little water and leave the jar somewhere warm for a week. When the beans have germinated, move the jar to somewhere light and watch the bean plants grow.

Germination

Seeds need three things to germinate, or start growing: water, air, and warmth. If all three are present, the seed can grow. Seeds do not need light to germinate.

To germinate, most seeds must be covered with a thin layer of soil. The first stage of germination is when the outer coating of the seed cracks and a tiny root grows downward into the soil. Next, a tiny shoot develops and grows upward. Once the shoot reaches the surface of the soil, leaves will start to appear. From then on, the plant will need light to grow.

key facts

- Most flowering plants grow from seeds.
- Seeds need air, water, and warmth to germinate.
- Seeds do not need light to germinate.

The growing plant

Growing plants get their energy from sunlight. This process is called **photosynthesis**.

Photosynthesis

Photosynthesis is a long word, but it can be split up into "photo," which means light, and "synthesis," which means making something. So photosynthesis actually means using light to make food. Green plants have a substance in them called **chlorophyll**. Chlorophyll is able to capture the energy in sunlight.

You can do it...

Find out the best conditions for growing seedlings. Put three seedlings in three separate pots. Place one in a dark place (a cupboard) and put the other two on a sunny windowsill. Water the one in the cupboard and only one of the plants on the windowsill regularly. Which seedling grows best?

In addition to sunlight, plants need water and the gas carbon dioxide for photosynthesis to happen. Water is taken in from the soil by the plant's roots and is then passed up the stem to the leaves. The plant's leaves absorb carbon dioxide from the air.

The process of photosynthesis creates glucose (a type of sugar), which the plant uses to develop and grow. It also produces the gas oxygen, which is released back into the air.

◄ Green leaves contain a substance called chlorophyll, which is able to turn the energy in sunlight into food for the plant.

Carbon dioxide is taken in from the air through tiny holes called **stomata**.

Light energy comes from the sun.

▲ Flowering plants have leaves of many different shapes and sizes, but their purpose is the same—to carry out photosynthesis.

Oxygen is given off into the air through the stomata.

Water is taken in from the soil through the roots.

▲ The process of photosynthesis in a green plant.

key facts

- Photosynthesis is the process by which plants make food from sunlight.

- Green leaves contain chlorophyll, which enables photosynthesis to take place.

- Plants need light, water, and carbon dioxide to photosynthesize.

Stems and roots

Flowering plants are held up by their stems. Below ground, roots anchor the plants in place and absorb water and **minerals**.

Stems

The stem of a plant is above ground. It has three functions. First, it supports the leaves and flowers. The leaves need to be held out so that they can face the light. The second function of the stem is to carry water and **nutrients** to the leaves, flowers, and fruits of the plant. The water is carried in small channels called veins. Thirdly, the stem carries the glucose made by photo-synthesis (*see page 8*) from the leaves to the rest of plant.

Some stems are green and flexible; some, such as those in shrubs and trees, are woody and give extra support. A tree stem is called the trunk. Some large tree trunks can be as wide as a car.

◄ The stems of the field poppy are green and flexible. This allows the plant to move in the wind without breaking.

Roots

The roots of a plant are usually below the ground. Roots have two important uses. One is to anchor the plant in the ground and prevent it from falling over. The other is to collect water. Large roots divide into small rootlets that are covered with tiny root hairs. These root hairs collect water and pass it up through the roots and stem to the leaves. The water contains minerals and nutrients which the plant needs for healthy growth.

key facts

- Stems support the plant and carry water and minerals to the leaves.

- Roots anchor the plant and absorb water and minerals from the ground.

You can do it...

See how water travels through the veins in a plant's stem. Put some celery stalks into a jar containing water that has been colored with ink or with food coloring. After a few hours you will see the celery change color. If you cut across a celery stalk, you will see where the veins are in the stalk.

▶ Mangrove trees grow in thick, sticky mud. Their roots stick up above the mud so that they can absorb the oxygen they need to grow.

Leaves

Leaves come in many shapes and sizes, but their main function is the same: to carry out photosynthesis and make food for the plant.

Leaves are a plant's factory, where the production of food takes place. Throughout the hours of daylight, the leaves are making sugars to feed the whole plant and provide it with the energy it needs to grow.

Structure of a leaf

Most leaves are flat and thin and designed to catch as much sunlight as possible. Simple leaves have just one leaf blade and a leaf stalk.

Compound leaves are made up of several leaflets growing out from a leaf stalk.

In a simple leaf there is one large vein called the midrib, which branches out into smaller veins covering the leaf.

▲ A compound leaf is made up of several small leaflets growing off the main leaf stalk.

▼ A cross-section of a typical leaf.

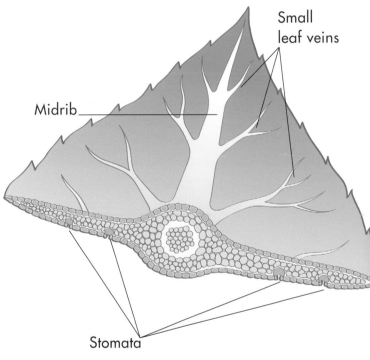

Small leaf veins

Midrib

Stomata

These veins carry water and minerals to the leaf and take away the sugars made by photosynthesis. On the underside of the leaf are many tiny holes called stomata. Gases pass in and out of the leaf through the stomata. The water which has moved through the plant's root and leaf system is also passed out through the stomata as **water vapor**.

You can do it...

Find out for yourself that plants give off water vapor. You will need a fairly small, leafy houseplant. Cover the plant with a clear plastic bag and tie it loosely around the stem. Leave the plant in a sunny place for a few hours. When you return you should be able to see tiny water droplets in the bag. They have been released by the plant.

Special features of leaves

Some plants have developed leaves with special features to suit the conditions in which they grow. On mountains, furry leaves keep out the strong sunlight. Plants that live in areas of heavy rain have to protect themselves from getting water-logged. One way they do this is to have waxy leaves with grooves that channel the water quickly off the leaf.

▲ In autumn, leaves on **deciduous** trees die and turn red, yellow, and gold. The tree then becomes **dormant** for the winter.

key facts

- Photosynthesis is carried out in the leaves of a plant.

- Leaves take in and pass out gases through holes called stomata.

- Leaves die and fall off deciduous trees in autumn.

◄ Plants that grow in still or slow-moving water sometimes have wide leaves that float on the surface. The Amazon water-lily produces huge leaves that can be more than two yards (1.8 m) around.

Flowers

Flowers come in many beautiful shapes and colors. Their purpose, however, is to produce the seeds that will one day grow into new plants.

The first flowers appeared on Earth about 100 million years ago. Now there are more than 250,000 species of flowering plants. Their flowers range from complex examples such as orchids and lilies to the simple **catkins** of some trees.

The structure of a flower

A flower is made up of several layers. A flower bud is covered with a layer of green sepals which protect it. When the flower opens it reveals petals, which are usually brightly colored and may have other markings. In the center are the male and female parts the flower needs in order to make seeds.

▼ The parts of a flower.

Style

Stamen

Stigma

Anther containing pollen

Petal

Ovary

Egg cells

Sepal

You can do it...

Look at a flower and see if you can identify all the parts shown above. Different flowers may have different numbers of petals, anthers, and stigmas, but you should be able to see them clearly.

◄ The catkin of the great sallow tree. The stamens are tipped with yellow pollen.

Male and female

The male stamens are long stalks which carry a sac of pollen at the end called an anther. The female part, the ovary, is at the base of the flower, with the style and stigma above it. The male cells are in the pollen; the female egg cells are in the ovary. To make a seed, the male and female cells need to join together.

▲ The lily is one of the most colorful of all flowers. It also has a beautiful scent.

▼ The flower heads of some plants, such as this daisy, are made up of small flowers called florets. In a daisy, one "head" of a flower can be made up of hundreds of florets. Each floret behaves like a flower and produces one seed.

key facts

- Flowers are the reproductive parts of a plant.

- Flowers carry male cells in the pollen and female cells in the ovary.

- Male and female cells join together to make seeds.

Pollination

Pollination happens when the male cells in the pollen are carried to the female parts of another plant.

To produce a seed, the male cells in the pollen must **fertilize** a female egg in the ovary. It is usually better if a flower is not fertilized by its own pollen, so the pollen has to be carried from the anthers of one plant to the stigma of another. Some flowering plants are pollinated by wind, while others rely on water or animals.

Wind pollination

Wind-pollinated plants produce a huge amount of pollen. Each catkin, or flower, on a birch tree can contain 5.5 million pollen grains. A single tree may have several thousand catkins. Imagine how much pollen is produced by all the birch trees in a forest! They need to produce so much pollen because only a very small amount of it will actually find the female parts of another birch tree.

▶ A hazel catkin in the process of shedding its pollen to be carried off by the wind. The flowers on wind-pollinated plants are often dull in color; they do not need to attract insects to pollinate them.

◄ Wind-pollinated plants such as grasses and trees grow together in large numbers to increase the chances of their pollen reaching another plant.

key facts

- Pollination happens when pollen from the male part of one plant is carried to the female part of another plant.

- Some flowers are pollinated by wind or water.

- Wind-pollinated plants produce an enormous quantity of pollen.

Pollen grains carried by the wind must travel long distances, so they are very small, light, and smooth to drift along on the breeze. The wind can take the grains up as high as 20,000 feet (6,000 m) and carry them more than 2,000 miles (3,200 km) from the parent plants.

Water pollination

Some plants are pollinated by water, and the pollen is dispersed downstream by rivers or streams. The *Elodea*, or Canadian pondweed, has stamens that grow under-water and release pollen that floats to the surface. The female flower (*right*) grows on the surface of the water and collects the pollen as it floats by.

Animal pollination

A flower's bright color, delicious scent, and the food it offers attract many animals, especially insects.

An animal visiting the flower may accidentally pick up some pollen on its body. When it then visits another flower of the same species, some of the pollen may rub off onto that flower's stigma. The plant has used the animal to help pollination take place.

◀ The most specialized of all nectar-feeding birds are the tiny hummingbirds.

Nectar

Bees and other insects eat pollen, but some plants also produce another food, nectar, to attract pollinators. Nectar is a sugary liquid that many animals seem to enjoy. In Africa, sunbirds, sugar birds, and honey-eaters are nectar-feeders, eating almost nothing else. They are all so small that they can perch on the flower itself.

▲ The tiny Australian honey possum lives entirely on nectar and pollen. It feeds with a long tongue that reaches deep into flowers. Its fur becomes covered with pollen, which rubs off on the next flower it visits.

◀ A painted lady butterfly feeds on the nectar from a thistle.

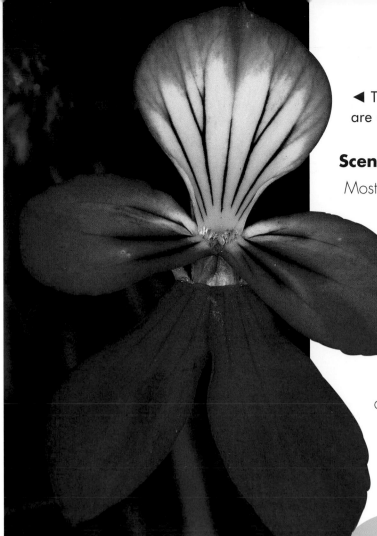

◄ The lines that guide insects to the nectar are clearly visible on this mountain pansy.

Scents

Most scents produced by flowers are attractive to insects and people alike. We use such flowers as lily of the valley, lavender, and rose to make perfumes and soaps. A few flowering plants have particularly nasty smells, yet the effect is the same: insects are attracted to them and pollination is successful.

key facts

- Insects, birds, small mammals, and lizards can pollinate flowers.

- Animals are attracted to flowers by their color, their scents, and the food they provide.

- Some petals have markings that guide pollinators to the right part of the flower.

Patterns

The spectacular colors of flowers are designed to attract insects. Some are also patterned in a way that guides the insects straight to where the plant wants them. Foxgloves, irises, and pansies, for example, have guidelines that lead from the outer edge of the petal down to the center of the flower. These marks are not unlike the guidelines we use on runways for landing airplanes. The insects follow them to reach the nectar. Some insects can actually see ultra-violet markings on flowers that are invisible to us.

From pollen to seed

A grain of pollen landing on the stigma of another plant is the first stage in the process of making a seed.

The next stage is that a pollen tube grows out of the pollen grain, down the style and into the ovary. Male sex cells travel down the pollen tube and join with female sex cells, the eggs in the ovary. The formation of seeds is called fertilization. After fertilization, the ovary gets bigger and turns into the fruit. The fruit's job is to protect the seeds and allow them to ripen.

Dispersing the seeds

When seeds are ripe, the plant needs to get them as far away as possible from itself to allow them to grow into healthy new plants. Young trees, for example, would not grow well in the shade of a fully-grown tree.

▲ These are the wind-dispersed seeds of the sycamore tree.

Wind dispersal

Some trees produce seeds with wings that allow them to fly far away from the parent plant. The wing-like seeds of ash trees and sycamores, for example, can travel long distances across the countryside like tiny helicopters.

The seeds of the poppy (a flower) are dispersed by the wind in a different way. As the wind blows, the seeds are shaken out of the dry hollow fruit, like pepper out of a shaker. The seeds are small and light, so they are carried easily by the wind.

You can do it...

Collect as many different types of seed as you can. Can you tell which ones are dispersed by wind and which ones by animals?

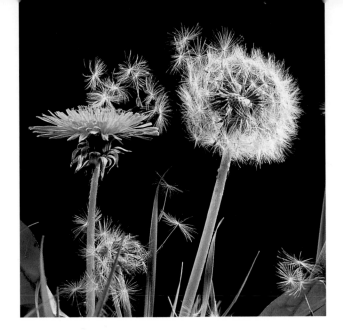

▲ The dandelion is an example of a flower that uses wind to disperse its seeds.

Animal dispersal

Fruits have bright colors and smells, and many of them taste good. This makes them attractive to hungry birds and animals. The seeds in a fruit are not digested by the animals and are passed out in their droppings. In this way, the animal has helped to move the seeds away from the parent plant.

Some seeds are covered in tiny hooks. These catch on to the fur of a passing animal so the seed is carried elsewhere.

Water dispersal

The coconut (*below*) is a seed that is dispersed by water. It has a massive store of food that will last it for a year. This allows the young coconut plant to survive on beaches where there is little fresh water. In this way, coconut trees can spread from one **tropical** island to another.

key facts

- Fertilization is when a male sex cell from a pollen grain joins with a female sex cell in the ovary of a plant.

- The fruit protects the seeds.

- Seeds can be dispersed by water, wind, or animals.

Life cycle of a sunflower

The easiest way to understand the stages in the life of a flowering plant is to follow its life cycle, starting with a seed.

Sunflowers are annual plants. This means they grow from seed each year. The seeds are large and striped. The first stage of growth is when the seed germinates and sends a rootlet down into the soil and a green shoot upward.

Sunflower plants grow quickly, at the rate of about four-tenths of an inch (1 cm) a day. The tip of the shoot grows the most. Sunflower stems are strong because they have to support a tall plant.

The sunflower's first leaves are called seed leaves. They contain a food store for the plant until the true leaves take over.

The growing plant

The leaves open out flat and wide to catch the sun. Once established, the energy produced by the leaves is put into growing flowers. At first, the flower buds are protected by sturdy green sepals.

You can do it...

Grow your own sunflowers. Plant some sunflower seeds and identify the stages of the life cycle as they grow.

▼ Stages in the growth of a sunflower seed. The shoot breaks through the soil and sheds its seed covering. The young plant then grows toward the light.

Pollination

The bright yellow petals of the sunflower, and the nectar it produces, attract various insects. These crawl all over the sunflower's face, moving pollen from one floret to another. In this way, the flowers are pollinated and seed growth is started. A sunflower head contains hundreds of seeds. Each one can grow another sunflower the following year.

▲ A bee crawls across the face of a sunflower, carrying pollen from one floret to another.

▼ Sunflower seeds are a valuable source of oil. Farmers grow sunflowers so that they can harvest the seeds. The seeds are crushed to remove the oil, which is used in cooking.

key facts

- Sunflowers are annual plants; they grow from seed each year.

- The flower of a sunflower is made up of many tiny florets.

- Sunflower seeds contain a useful cooking oil.

Special adaptations

Plants are found on every continent of the world and have developed a range of **adaptations** to cope with almost all conditions.

Saving water

About 10,000 species (types) of flowering plants are succulents. These plants live in very dry places and have developed a structure different from other plants. Euphorbias and cacti store water in their fleshy stems. Their roots absorb water rapidly, and their stems can expand quickly when water is available.

Succulents have no leaves, which minimizes water loss. Their stems are adapted to do the job of photosynthesis.

Avoiding predators

Plants cannot move away from animals that might eat them, so they have developed several forms of protection. Some plants are covered with spines or thorns to deter browsing animals. Others, such as the stinging nettle, are protected by fine hairs that sting.

Some plants contain a poison that discourages animals from eating them. Young bracken leaves are filled with the poison cyanide. When the leaves are older, not only are they too tough for most animals to eat, but they also contain poisons that can cause blindness and **cancer** in mammals.

◄ The spiny stems of this euphorbia store water. The spines protect the plant from being eaten.

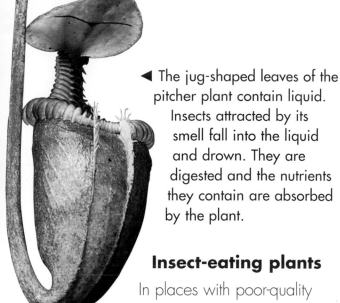

◄ The jug-shaped leaves of the pitcher plant contain liquid. Insects attracted by its smell fall into the liquid and drown. They are digested and the nutrients they contain are absorbed by the plant.

Insect-eating plants

In places with poor-quality soil, some plants get extra nutrients by trapping insects with their leaves. The pitcher plant has special leaves that grow into jug-like pitchers. These contain water and **digestive juices**. If an insect falls into the pitcher, it drowns and is digested and absorbed by the plant over a period of several days.

Parasitic plants

About one percent of all flowering plants are parasitic. This means they steal some of their food from other plants. The plants they live on are called hosts. Mistletoe is a parasitic plant that grows on trees.

► The Venus flytrap has hinged leaves that snap shut on any insect that lands on them. It takes between 8 and 20 days for a Venus flytrap to digest an insect.

key facts

○ Plants can protect themselves from predators with spines, stings, and poison.

○ Some plants can trap animals and gain extra nourishment from them.

○ A small number of flowering plants are parasitic.

◄ The sticky white berries of mistletoe are eaten by birds. As the birds wipe their beaks on the bark, the seeds are spread to other tree trunks.

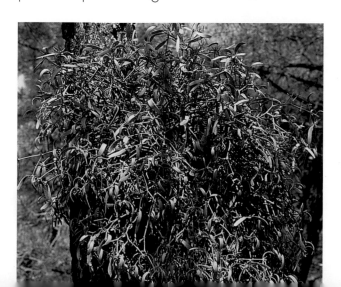

Unusual flowers

Most flowers are fairly small, with bright colors and a sweet smell, but there are exceptions.

▲ A rafflesia flower opens out on the forest floor in Sumatra, Indonesia.

Largest flower

The largest flower in the world is the rafflesia parasite, which lives in the rainforests of Borneo and Sumatra. The plant actually lives inside the roots of a vine. At certain times of the year, a lump grows out of the vine root and for several weeks gets bigger and bigger.

Eventually five leaves unfold, revealing a huge, orange, leathery flower that can be over a yard (91 cm) in diameter. The flower smells of rotting meat and attracts small flies which pollinate it. After three or four days, the flower collapses and disappears, leaving behind a small, woody fruit.

Nastiest flower

The dead horse arum grows on the islands of Corsica and Sardinia in the Mediterranean. Its appearance and smell make it one of the nastiest flowers around. It grows near colonies of gulls and produces its one flower at the height of the birds' breeding season. The flower is grayish-purple, streaked with pink, and about 10 inches (25 cm) across. It looks and smells like rotting flesh.

A gull colony is full of blowflies that are attracted to broken and rotting eggs. The blowflies crawl into the center of the arum flower to search for the source of the smell. In this way they pollinate the flower.

▲ The vile-smelling flower of the dead horse arum attracts blowflies, which help it to pollinate.

Fastest-growing flower

The titan arum is another giant flower from Sumatra. This flower grows at enormous speed, pushing upward at the rate of about four inches (10 cm) a day. The final flower stands about four and a half yards (3 m) tall, but lasts for only two days.

key facts

- The largest flower in the world is the rafflesia.
- The titan arum is the fastest-growing flower.
- Some flowers smell of rotting meat to attract pollinators.

Plants and people

People need plants. We could not live without the food they provide, the oxygen they create, or the numerous other things we obtain from them and use to make our lives better.

Food

All humans and animals rely on plants for food. Most of the things we eat come from plants. Large areas of the world are farmed to produce crops to feed people or animals.

On the prairies of North America, farmers grow grain crops such as wheat, corn, and barley. In Asia, rice is the **staple** grain crop. Tropical areas that have lots of sun and rain yield fruits such as bananas, pineapples, mangoes, and papaya.

▼ In southeast Asia, rice is grown in flooded fields called paddies, and is the staple food for millions of people.

▲ Timber is one of the most useful plant products. Wood can be used to build houses and make furniture, or burned for cooking and to provide warmth.

Wood

Trees provide us with wood, which has many uses. Wood is strong and light. It can be cut easily and can also be carved. Wood is very valuable for building and is the most popular material for making furniture.

◄ The drug digitalis, used to treat heart disease, comes from a flower called the foxglove.

Fuel

Plants provide us with fuel. In many areas of the world, people use wood for cooking and to provide heat.

The fossil fuels of coal, oil, and natural gas are all formed from the remains of prehistoric plants and animals. They are extracted from the ground and burned in power plants to generate electricity.

Paper

Paper is made from wood. Each person uses one tree's worth of paper every year. Rubber and cork also come from trees. Cork is the thick, spongy bark of the cork oak tree, and rubber comes from the **sap** that is collected from rubber trees.

Textiles

Many of the materials we use for making clothes come from plants. Cotton is the most commonly used **natural fiber**. It is made from the cotton plant, and it is used for bed sheets, curtains, clothes, tablecloths, towels, and many other purposes.

Medicines

For thousands of years people have known about the medicinal qualities of certain plants. A 60,000-year-old burial site in Iraq was found to contain the remains of eight different medicinal plants. Although many medicines today are made from chemicals, plant remedies still remain a valuable source of drugs.

key facts

- Without plants we could not survive.
- Plants provide us with food, fuel, and building materials.
- Many plants have important medicinal qualities.

Glossary

Adaptation The way in which animals and plants change over many generations to survive better in their particular environment.

Cancer A disease that affects cells in the body, causing tumors to grow. Many people die of cancer each year.

Catkins The primitive flowers of some wind-pollinated trees.

Chlorophyll The green pigment found in plant leaves that absorbs light during the process of photosynthesis.

Coniferous A type of plant that produces seeds inside cones instead of flowers.

Deciduous A type of tree that sheds its leaves in autumn.

Digestive juices The juices produced by an insect-eating plant that break down food into substances that can be absorbed and used by the plant.

Dormant Something that is not growing or being active.

Fertilization The joining together of the male and female cells to make a new plant.

Minerals Naturally occurring substances that are found in the ground. Minerals are needed for the healthy growth of plants and animals.

Natural fibers Materials that occur naturally on Earth—usually obtained from plants or animals.

Nutrients Substances that help animals and plants grow better.

Photosynthesis The method by which plants make food from sunlight, water, and carbon dioxide.

Sap The watery liquid in plants.

Species A group of plants or animals that look alike and can breed with each other successfully.

Staple Main, or basic part of something.

Stomata The tiny openings in a leaf through which gases and water vapor pass.

Tropical Describes the part of the world between the Tropic of Cancer and the Tropic of Capricorn surrounding the Equator.

Water vapor Water in the form of a gas.

Further information

Books

Batten, Mary. *Hungry Plants*. New York: Random Library, 2004.

Harwood, Penny. *Meat-Eating Plants*. New York: McGraw Hill Children's Publishing, 2003.

Worth, Bonnie. *Oh Say Can You Seed: All About Flowering Plants*. New York: Random House, 2001.

Web sites

Biology4Kids.com
Angiosperms and Flowering Plants. Read up on these flowering plants and find out what dicots and monocots are!
http://www.biology4kids.com/files/plants_angiosperm.html

The Butterfly House
This site provides step-by-step directions for creating a butterfly garden.
http://www.butterflyhouse.org/gardening.html

Photosynthesis, Energy, and Life
This site tells about photosynthesis and other energy sources that move through nature.
http://www.ftexploring.com/photosyn/photosynth.html

Angiosperms
Learn about these flowering plants that make up the largest group in the plant kingdom.
http://pittsford.monroe.edu/jefferson/calfieri/plants/Angiosperm.html

Places to Visit

U.S.
American Museum of Natural History
New York City, New York
http://www.amnh.org

Field Museum of Natural History
Chicago, Illinois
http://www.fieldmuseum.org

Heard Natural Science Museum and Wildlife Sanctuary
McKinney, Texas
http://www.heardmuseum.org

Pacific Science Center
Seattle, Washington
http://www.pacsci.org

Smithsonian Institution
Washington, DC
http://www.si.edu

Canada
Canadian Museum of Nature
Victoria Memorial Museum Building
Ottawa, Ontario
http://www.nature.ca

Provincial Museum of Alberta
Edmonton, Alberta
http://www.pma.edmonton.ab.ca

Index